Grammar Repair Kit
Improve Your
Grammar Skills

ANGELA BURT
WILLIAM VANDYCK

Hodder
Children's
Books

a division of Hachette Children's Books

CONTENTS

INTRODUCTION

GRAMMAR
THE BIG QUESTION: WHY BOTHER?

This is easy.

Try this free quiz:

FREE QUIZ

You write something for an exam, or for a job, or to a friend. For anything. Would you rather seem:

a) not stupid

b) stupid.

Would you prefer people to:

a) understand you?

b) think you are stupid?

OK – aaaaand time's up, stop.

HOW DID YOU DO?

Mostly "b"s. Fine. That's great. You can put this book down and go and play. Or pop into the next room to see if you're there. Or watch some paint dry. Really. Have a good life. Bye! Have you gone yet?

Mostly "a"s. OK. Then you need to know about grammar. Let's leave Stupid ironing his pants and see why.

INTRODUCTION

Grammar is about how we put words together to say what we mean.

It's not enough just to know the words you want to use. For a start, you need to know what order to put the words in. You don't say:

Jake buried the octopus. if you mean **The octopus buried Jake.**

What's more, getting the order of the words correct isn't enough if you don't use the right ones. If you want to say:

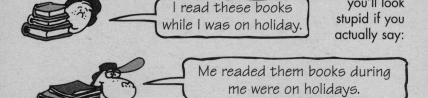

I read these books while I was on holiday.

you'll look stupid if you actually say:

Me readed them books during me were on holidays.

Finally, getting the wrong word can completely change the meaning of what you say, even if it sounds like it should be OK. For example:

The captain of the ship which was 10 metres wide, carried four aircraft and was made of hard grey steel was smiling.

means:

But

The captain of the ship who was 10 metres wide, carried four aircraft and was made of hard grey steel was smiling.

means:

So, you need to know about grammar. OK?

NOW FOR SOME GOOD NEWS.

We're going to try to avoid using unnecessary jargon. So you won't have to remember about:

the third person singular

the third person plural

the third person's penpal

the third person's poodle

the third person's puddle

the third person's penpal's
poodle paddling in a puddle

And there's some other good news, too...

INTRODUCTION

You are not alone. There's the enormous ghost standing behind you, for a start. Just kidding. Actually, here in the Grammar Repair Kit garage there's Zelda. Say hi, Zelda.

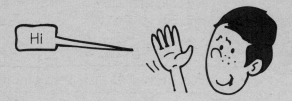

And there's Steven, the Stupid Monster. Say hello, Steven.

Oh, dear. And there's Colin.

Hello. I want to be a teacher, and I'm going to practise on you. Some people say I'm dull. 23 of them. Today, anyway. I keep count, you see, in a little notebook. Well, anyway, I'm really very interesting. Perhaps the most interesting gravel collector I know. And I'm going to liven things up with some "jokes" every now and again.

Er, great. I'm sure that's something we're all looking forward to, Colin.

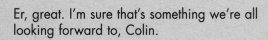

Can I just say I know about Grammar. I see her every Christmas.

No, Steven, that's Grandma. And anyway, there's no time to say that. We've got to make a start.

Let's go to work.

NOUNS

You've probably heard the term **NOUN** before.
Can you remember what nouns do?

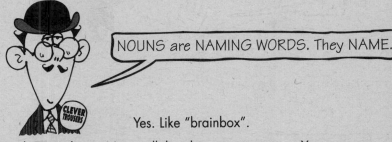

NOUNS are NAMING WORDS. They NAME.

CLEVER TROUSERS

Yes. Like "brainbox".

Look around you. Name all the objects you can see. You are using NOUNS.

Name all the people in your class. You are using NOUNS.

Make a list of the presents you would like for your next birthday. You are using NOUNS.

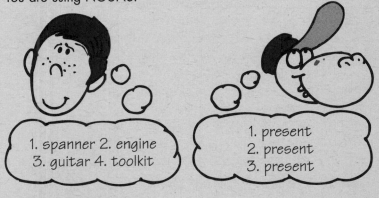

1. spanner 2. engine 3. guitar 4. toolkit

1. present
2. present
3. present

Now, you may wonder ...

Why is it important to KNOW about nouns if I've been using them perfectly well ever since I first learned to talk?

Why baby

Quite. Well. Colin – help us out here.

Firstly, it's quite interesting.

Secondly, if you know a bit more about nouns then you'll know if they need capital letters or not when you write them and you'll know whether they're singular or plural so that you can make the rest of the sentence match and you'll learn lots of new words.

Thirdly, it helps to know about your own language when you want to learn someone else's like French or German or Italian or Spanish. They have nouns too.

Fourthly, it's the sort of thing your teacher likes you to know about so that you can do well in the SATs. So there are lots of reasons, Zelda.

Zelda?

Zelda's off to have fun with words, including nouns. Let's join her.

Don't confuse the following:

noun: hat, bird

nun:

nan:

nan bread:

hey nonny no:

In the end, it's like this:

**1.   Person who knows
about nouns.**

**2.   Person who doesn't know
about nouns.**

You choose.

COMMON NOUNS

Common nouns are the names of objects.

Play "I Spy" for a moment. See how many things you can see beginning with b. All these will be common nouns.

I spy with my little eye: eyelid, eyelid, eyelid, eyelid.

General words like boy, girl, teacher, parent are common nouns as well.

FIND THE WORDS – WIN A TROPHY!*
(common nouns)

Find ten articles of clothing in this wordsearch:
anorak, boots, gloves, jeans, sandals, scarf, socks, sweater, tie, trousers.

```
T A N O R A K D
R I M S O C K S
O L E D N F A E
U S A N D A L S
S C A R F R E P
E S E V O L G J
R B O O T S K O
S W E A T E R Y
```

The answers are all in the back of the book.

* This bit's not true. No trophy. Sorry.

GOING TO THE DOGS: NAME THE BREED
(all common nouns)

1. a l _ _ _ i a n

4. b _ _ _ d o g

2. p _ _ _ l e

5. s _ _ _ i e l

3. s _ _ _ _ d o g

ALPHABET PUZZLE: A IS FOR ARACHNOPHOBE

Think of 26 common nouns, each beginning with a different letter of the alphabet. The zanier your word the better.

a
b
c
d
e
f
g
h
i
j
k
l
m
n
o
p
q
r
s
t
u
v
w
x
y
z

Make sure all the words are common nouns.

There's a musical instrument beginning with xylo . . .

COMPOUND NOUNS:
two for the price of one!!!

Have you ever noticed that some common nouns are really two
nouns joined together? I'm thinking of words like
cupboard, armchair, handkerchief, bedroom, doughnut.
We call these **compound nouns** but they're still common nouns
as well.

I'm a rattlesnake.
I'm a **compound**
common noun.

Yeah, dead
common, love.

Compound nouns start by being written as two separate words
when they're used together a lot:

a school bus
a washing machine
a boy band

In your lifetime, you'll probably see them begin to be written with a
hyphen. It usually takes years and years before this happens. Some
dictionaries will quickly include them with the hyphen; others will
go on listing them in the old two-word way.

In my dictionary, these compound nouns are now listed with a hyphen:

taxi-driver
motor-bike
crash-helmet

Eventually, they'll probably be written as single words.
Or, if you're reading this in the year 2090 – "singlewords".

Check in your dictionary how these words are written:

hair brush	hair-brush	hairbrush
table cloth	table-cloth	tablecloth
shop keeper	shop-keeper	shopkeeper
head ache	head-ache	headache
fire guard	fire-guard	fireguard

COLIN'S CONCLUSIONS PAGE

=pancake

Look, Steven, if you can't work out where "pancake" comes from within another 15 seconds, I'm going to suggest we move on to "peabrain".

PROPER NOUNS

Proper nouns are the individual names of people, pets, towns, countries, clubs and organisations, and so on. They always begin with a capital letter.

COMMON NOUNS	PROPER NOUNS
girl	Kayleigh
town	Exmouth
dog	Spot

I'm **Colin** (proper noun). I am a **boy** (common noun). I want to be a **teacher** (common noun).

That's quite enough of that, **idiot** (common noun)!

Make your answers start with a capital S-s-s-s-s-s.

IT'S ONLY PROPER, INNIT?

1. Name a country.   S_____

2. Name a town.   S_____

3. Name a planet.   S_____

4. Name a mountain.   S_____

5. Name a river.   S_____

6. Name a girl.   S_____

7. Name a boy.   S_____

HUNT THE PROPER NOUNS

Find the five nouns which are proper nouns and write them out properly with a capital letter at the beginning.

> manchester   pencil
>
>   doctor   village   wales
>
> chicken   oliver   basket
>
>   norway   everest
>
>   crisps   road

1. _____
2. _____
3. _____
4. _____
5. _____

GENERAL KNOWLEDGE QUIZ

1. Who wrote 'James and the Giant Peach'?

2. What was Shakespeare's first name?

3. What's the capital of Sweden?

4. Which Germanic god is Thursday named after?

5. Which month has 28 days? ***

*** Watch out! Question 5 is a ...

All the answers are proper nouns and begin with capital letters.

PROPER LITTLE DEVIL

COLLECTIVE NOUNS

Collective nouns are the names of collections of things like a **herd** of cows, a **bouquet** of flowers, an **anthology** of poems, a **swarm** of bees.

COLLECTIVE STRENGTH TEST

Do you know the missing collective nouns?

1. a _____ of sheep
2. a _____ of ships
3. a _____ of stars
4. a _____ of fish
5. a _____ of thieves

You can have fun making up collective nouns. We haven't got enough in the language!

MAKE UP YOUR OWN COLLECTIVE NOUNS – WIN A TROPHY*

1. a _____ of teachers
2. a _____ of skeletons
3. a _____ of bicycles
4. a _____ of rock bands
5. a _____ of computers

a **cuddle** of kittens

a **squelching** of tadpoles

a **wetness** of kisses

a **hatstand** of hatstands

a problem of bad breath

* Not true here, either. Sorry.

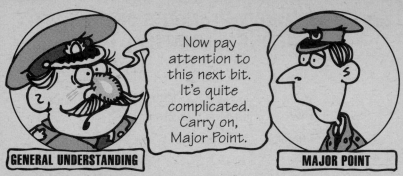

Now pay attention to this next bit. It's quite complicated. Carry on, Major Point.

GENERAL UNDERSTANDING

MAJOR POINT

COLLECTIVE NOUNS ARE SINGULAR (unless you make them plural).

Here is an example.

You should say: a **swarm** of bees **has** landed on Colin's head. ✓

You shouldn't say:
a **swarm** of bees **have** landed on Colin's head. ✗

I agree.

If you like, you can make **swarm** plural. You can change it into **swarms**. Then you can say "have landed".
Swarms of bees **have** landed on
Colin's head.

No, don't say that! Help!

YOU

STOP

IT'S TIME TO TEST YOUR UNDERSTANDING!

TEST YOUR UNDERSTANDING OF THIS VERY ADVANCED GRAMMATICAL POINT

1. A herd of cows _____ eating your lawn. Ha ha! (is/are)

2. A bouquet of flowers _____ presented to the winner of the "Don't kill flowers" competition. (was/were)

3. That suite of furniture _____ too bouncy to be safe. (is/are)

4. Crowds of fans _____ at the concert. (was/were)

5. A large crowd of supporters _____ shouting slogans.(was/were)

We only sing when we're singing. Sing when we're singing...

AND NOW HEAR THIS:

You are the secretary of the General, who isn't quite sure which words to use where he has put alternatives. Can you say which words is/are correct – by teatime?

MEMO TO TROOPS:

The army which is/are going on these missions should be aware that they will be dangerous. Neither success, nor glory, nor a filling packed lunch is guaranteed. It may very well be that this brave troop is/are unlikely to want to go if there is no packed lunch. I understand. But anyone in this army who is not willing to go just for that reason should give his or her name to me and I will try to cadge some sandwiches and cubes of cheese and Penguin biscuits for them.

I would wish to make sure that this rabble realise/realises that the whole thing is not just about food, you know. Many have mentioned this issue to me. But if just a few of you were more interested in getting out there and fighting rather than stuffing your faces all the time, I wouldn't be known as "Lardyguts" Understanding at the club.

Yours **General "Lardyguts" Understanding**

ABSTRACT NOUNS

Abstract nouns are the names of feelings, thoughts and concepts. You can't hold them in your hand. You can't smell them. You can't hear them or see them.

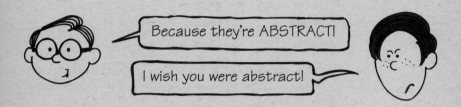

Because they're ABSTRACT!

I wish you were abstract!

Here are some abstract nouns.

kindness	sympathy
affection	love
fear	freedom
childhood	generosity

Abstract nouns have a lot of different endings. Here are some of them:

-ness	-dom	-ty	-ion	-ice
-hood	-our	-ship	-ment	-ure

Choose the right ending for these abstract nouns.

1. friend _____
2. nervous _____
3. boy _____
4. king _____
5. loyal _____
6. excite _____
7. just _____
8. fail _____
9. cruel _____
10. gentle _____

Sometimes abstract nouns are quite difficult to spell because you don't just have to add an ending. You have to change the word in other ways as well.

For example:

high	height
wise	wisdom
silent	silence
sincere	sincerity

You'll get to know the common ones. Use a dictionary if you're not sure.

TESTING TESTING ONE TWO THREE FOUR.
OH, YOU GET THE GENERAL IDEA.

Change these words into abstract nouns.

1. lonely   ness
2. miserable   y
3. confident   ce
4. generous   ity
5. cowardly   ice
6. lazy   Actually, don't bother with this one.

Fill in the missing letters in these abstract nouns.

7. proud   pr _ _ _
8. wide   wi _ _ _
9. brave   brav _ _ _
10. noble   nob _ _ _ _ _
11. beautiful   b _ _ _ _ _

GENERAL POINTS ABOUT NOUNS
GENDER

Nouns are said to be masculine if they refer to males. When are nouns said to be masculine, Steven?

When they refer to males.

Correct, for example: **boy**, **father**, **uncle**, **stallion**, **cockerel**.

Nouns are said to be feminine if they refer to females. When are nouns feminine, Steven?

When they refer to females.

That's right – **girl**, **mother**, **aunt**, **mare**, **hen**.

Nouns are said to be common if they refer to both male and female. When are they said to be common?

When they refer to both male and female.

Right – eg **child**, **parent**, **relation**, **horse**, **fowl**.

Don't confuse this meaning of the word "common" with "common nouns" as explained on page 8.

Nouns are said to be neuter if they refer to objects: **pen**, **table**, **fork**, **spoon**.

When are nouns said to be neuter, Steven?

When they refer to objects.

Yeah. Steven is said to be stupid if he asks, "When do I get a pie in my face?"

When do I get a pie in my face?

Now!

GENDER-AL KNOWLEDGE

Sort these nouns into the four gender columns (masculine, feminine, common and neuter).

nun   chair   nephew   judge   ram   book

telephone   bull   heiress   doctor   desk   daughter

grandfather   pet   queen   teacher

STAND-INS

Find words of common gender that can take the place of these masculine and feminine nouns:

1. headmistress

2. clergyman

3. foreman

4. policeman

5. spokesman

YOU DON'T HAVE TO KNOW THIS BUT...

Listen out for people referring to things like cars or ships as if they were female.

> She's been a wonderful ship, and never let me drown before.

> She's a bit old and battered, bad at starting in the morning and high-maintenance, but my own car's OK.

SINGULAR AND PLURAL

Singular means ONE of something.

Plural means MORE THAN ONE.

AAAAAaarghh!

It's OK, Zelda, you were just having bad dreams.

Be careful with the spelling when you make nouns plural. This is the general rule:

MOST WORDS ADD -S OR -ES TO FORM THE PLURAL.

But, yes, you've guessed it. That's not the end of the story.
And you know what they say, the story ain't over till the fat lady sings.

You mean isn't.

CLEVER TROUSERS

La!

Not yet, Fat Lady – do try to pay attention.

Oh, sorry, there's more about plurals than just adding -s or -es, isn't there?

Yes Ye-s Y-es!

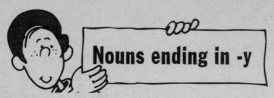

Nouns ending in -y

Nouns ending in vowel +y add -s

(e.g. monkey monkeys)

Nouns ending in consonant +y change the y to i before adding -es

(e.g. lady ladies)

Nouns ending in -o

Nouns ending in -o usually add -s but there are some important exceptions like potato**es** and tomato**es**.

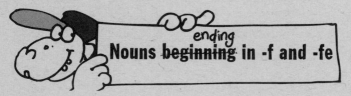

Nouns beginning ~~beginning~~ ending in -f and -fe

Nouns ending in -f and -fe usually add -s but sometimes you have to remember to change the f to v (as in half – hal**v**es and wife – wi**v**es) before adding –**e**s.

And there are still more irregular plurals to remember.

Regular soldier

Irregular soldier

PECULIAR PLURALS

man	men
child	children
woman	women
mouse	mice
louse	lice

EVEN MORE PECULIAR PLURALS

goose	geese
tooth	teeth
foot	feet

GETTING VERY ODD NOW

cod	cod
trout	trout
salmon	salmon
sheep	sheep
deer	deer

STEADY I THINK SHE'S GONNA PANIC

oasis	oases
radius	radii
bacterium	bacteria
antenna	antennae

LOOK OUT EVERYBODY!

syllabus	syllabi or syllabuses
terminus	termini or terminuses

TRANCEOMETER

110
Colin says
something
interesting.

80
Dog sumo
wrestler
sues man.

60
Dog
sues
man.

40
Man
bites
dog.

20
Dog
bites
man.

AND... RELAX:

If the plural is irregular
(i.e. peculiar)
it will be in your
dictionary.

**So remember to look up spellings you're not
sure about.**

FIND THE PECULIAR PLURALS –
OR YOUR FAVOURITE THING EXPLODES

Find all six words with peculiar plurals in this wordsearch puzzle.
Then find two words in the singular – can you say what their
plurals should be?

```
E  S  E  E  G  E  N
S  E  M  R  E  E  D
U  S  A  L  M  O  N
O  A  N  O  C  E  E
M  O  W  T  E  E  F
```

Zelda – you're a singular kind of girl. Why don't I give you a
ringular later, and we'll go out and do somethingular.

Colin – go and work out
the plural of "No".

Nose?

USING THE POSSESSIVE APOSTROPHE

There is a strange, bad-tempered breed of monster called a Rophe.

One particular breed of Rophe likes crawling through people's letterboxes when they're eating breakfast. This breed was originally known as "a Post Rophe".

However, language has developed over the years (see page 10), and these monsters are now known as

APOSTROPHES.

And when people say that they don't know how to deal with an apostrophe (pronounced a-poss-tra-fee) it must be the little monster that looks like that that they're thinking about.

Because dealing with the apostrophe that looks like this ' is really easy when you know how!

You want to show that Zelda owns the spanner?
Is it:

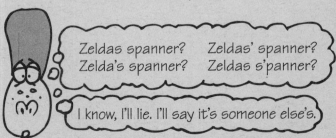

Zeldas spanner?   Zeldas' spanner?
Zelda's spanner?   Zeldas s'panner?

I know, I'll lie. I'll say it's someone else's.

No, you don't need to lie. The good news is there's a really easy way to get it right...

Stanley Savenergy's Ruler:

Of course he saves energy:
I do the measuring for him.

Stanley Savengery's Rule:

1. Name the owner.   Zelda

2. Put the apostrophe next.   Zelda'

3. If there isn't an s immediately
    before the apostrophe, add one.   Zelda's

4. Add the rest.   Zelda's spanner

Use it safely with plural words too, whether they're peculiar plurals
or not. Sometimes you'll end up with s' and sometimes with 's.
Everything will sort itself out if you follow the rule.

The cries of the babies

Name the owner.	babies
Put the apostrophe next.	babies'
If there isn't an s, add one.	(already got an s)
Add the rest.	babies' cries

The books of the children

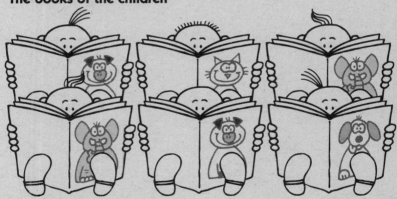

Name the owner.	children
Put the apostrophe next.	children'
If there isn't an s, add one.	children's
Add the rest.	children's books

COLIN'S CHALKBOARD CONCLUSIONS

NOUNS

1. Nouns are naming words.

2. There are four kinds of nouns: common, proper, collective and abstract.

3. Nouns can be masculine, feminine, neuter or common gender.

4. Most nouns form their plural by adding -s or -es (but BE CAREFUL!).

5. Possessive apostrophes are put directly after the owner's name.

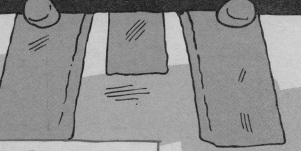

This is an announcer.

This is a noun, sir.

JUST MESSING ABOUT

Time to have a break!

Let's have some useless interesting information.

Tell us about eponyms.

EPONYM: the person that something is named after.

Example: Julius Caesar who gave his name to July.

Can you guess what was named after the following six people?

1. Jean Nicot (1530-1600), French diplomat, first introduced tobacco to France.

Not to be confused with Nick O'Tel, the famous hotel thief of the 1860s.

2. American president Theodore Roosevelt (1858-1919), nicknamed Teddy, once spared the life of a bear cub while out hunting.

Er... I will spare you.

3. Joseph Guillotin (1738-1814) gave his name to a machine which was used to behead people during the French Revolution.

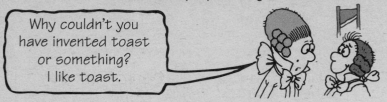

Why couldn't you have invented toast or something? I like toast.

4. Laszlo Biro (1900-1985), Hungarian inventor, made a pen with quick-drying ink which worked better at high altitudes than ordinary fountain pens and was used by the RAF during World War Two.

Can I borrow your Laszlo?

5. Lord Sandwich (1718-1792) was a dreadful gambler who begrudged time wasted at the dinner table. He preferred to eat a snack while he carried on gambling, usually a slice of beef between two slices of bread.

Actually there's another theory about that.

6. Joseph Cyril Bamford (b.1916) developed and manufactured an earth-moving machine with a huge scoop in the front operated hydraulically.

Look what I've invented, Mr B.U.L.L. Dozer.

Bah, now I'll never be famous.

PRONOUNS

Read this very boring letter written by one of Colin's friends.
(Actually it is so boring that we'll just ask you to read one page.)

> and then Zelda and Steven asked Colin if Colin would like
> Zelda and Steven to paint Colin a picture. Colin said that
> Zelda and Steven were very kind to offer to paint a picture
> for Colin but Colin was actually very good at painting and
> Colin thought that Colin could probably paint a better
> picture than Zelda and Steven could. Zelda and
> Steven were upset.

Wasn't that REALLY REALLY boring! It would be a bit better if all
that Zelda and Steven and Colin stuff could be cut down.

And it CAN! This is where PRONOUNS come in. Pronouns can do
the work of nouns by standing in for them.

> and then Zelda and Steven asked Colin if <u>he</u> would like <u>them</u>
> to paint <u>him</u> a picture. Colin said <u>they</u> were very kind to
> offer to paint a picture for <u>him</u> but <u>he</u> was actually very
> good at painting and <u>he</u> thought that <u>he</u> could probably paint
> a better picture than <u>they</u> could. <u>They</u> were upset.

Sure, it's still pretty dull (I did say it was a friend of Colin's), but at
least your head won't start to spin when reading it. The pronouns
that we've used here to replace the proper nouns Zelda, Steven
and Colin are personal pronouns. They are called personal
pronouns because they mostly refer to people.

I'm pro-bananas.

UP ME!

I'm pro-noun.

PERSONAL PRONOUNS

I	you	he	she	it	we	they

me	you	him	her	it	us	them

Personal pronouns come in pairs.

How do you know whether to use the one in the top box or the one in the bottom box?

It's easy.

Look at this example: **Zelda** kicks the ball.

Zelda is DOING the kicking. She is a DOER. Use a pronoun from the top box.

She kicks the ball.

Now look at this example: Colin kicks **Zelda**.

Zelda (poor thing!) is having the kicking DONE to her. Use a pronoun from the bottom box.

Colin kicks **her**.

I say! I NEVER would! That's not fair!

That's true. Let's think of a more likely example.

They kicked **him.**

CHOOSE THE RIGHT PRONOUN

1. My little brother is always annoying (I / me).
2. (We / us) love cooking.
3. My uncle didn't recognise (I / me).
4. (They / Them) collect spiders.
5. (She / Her) loves all animals.

A DIFFICULT BIT MADE A BIT LESS DIFFICULT

Some people find it very difficult deciding whether to use I or me in sentences like this:

My mother and ___ love chocolate.

The best thing to do is to think of it as two sentences before you make up your mind.

My mother loves chocolate.
I love chocolate.

My mother and **I** love chocolate. ✓

Here's another example:

The Queen has invited my friend and _____ to tea.

The Queen has invited my friend to tea.
The Queen has invited **me** to tea.

The Queen has invited my friend and **me** to tea. ✓

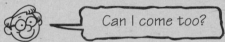
Can I come too?

No. This method works in sentences like this too.

The invitation has been given to you and _____.
The invitation has been given to you.
The invitation has been given to **me**.
The invitation has been given to you and **me**. ✓

CHOOSE I OR ME IN THESE SENTENCES

1. My friend and (I / me) are very sorry.
2. Let my friend and (I / me) off this time so we can do it again.
3. Please invite Sarah and (I / me) to your party. We do so want to snub you by not coming.
4. You and (I / me) will teach the bullies to crawl.
5. They'll have to crawl in order to get you and (I / me) out from under the bed.

"We don't tend to have this problem."

POSSESSIVE PRONOUNS

mine   yours   his   hers   ours   theirs

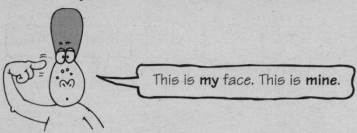

This is **my** face. This is **mine**.

Possessive pronouns show who owns something. They're easy to use BUT there is one important thing you have to remember.

POSSESSIVE PRONOUNS DON'T NEED APOSTROPHES

Quite right, Colin. Pronouns don't need them. They speak for themselves.

So you never write "your's" or "our's". No.

PUT THAT BISCUIT DOWN AND CHECK YOU UNDERSTAND THIS NOW, OK?

Use possessive pronouns instead of the underlined words.

1. That's <u>his lunchbox</u> not <u>your lunchbox</u>.

   That's _____ not _____.

2. The car was <u>their car</u> but now it's <u>my car</u>.

   The car was _____ but now it's _____.

Possessive pronouns speaking for themselves

Whose was the least successful team in the world?

Theirs.

REFLEXIVE PRONOUNS

Oh Colin! Have you hurt **yourself**?

Yes, the phone rang and it was a reflex action. I found I was ironing myself.

myself   yourself   himself   herself   itself
ourselves   yourselves   themselves

These pronouns are called reflexive pronouns. Colin thinks that they should be called "boomerang" pronouns because they always refer back to the DOER.

I wash **myself**.

You hurt **yourself**.

They dress **themselves**.

Be careful with the spelling. Don't make the mistakes that Steven makes.

ourselfs ✗
yourselfs ✗
theirselfs ✗
themselfs ✗

I haven't shown myself in the best light, have I?

You'll have to educate yourself.

Don't use **myself** when you need **I** or **me**.

My friend and ~~myself~~ like ice-cream.
My friend and **I** like ice-cream.

They invited my friend and ~~myself~~.
They invited my friend and **me**.

COLIN'S CHALKBOARD CONCLUSIONS

PRONOUNS

1. Pronouns take the place of nouns.

2. Personal pronouns come in pairs. Be careful to choose the right one of the pair.

3. Possessive pronouns don't need apostrophes.

I "pronoun"ce you "she" and "he".

How do you pronounce "He is Dull"?

I give up, how do you pronounce "He is Dull?"

Never mind.

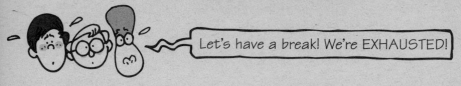

JUST MESSING ABOUT

Let's have a break! We're EXHAUSTED!

Good idea! Let's take a break and find out where some of the words in our language come from.

break: a pause for rest   (Old English <u>brecan</u> = to break)

exhausted: tired out   (Latin <u>exhaustus</u> = drained dry)

Can you match up these words with where they have come from? The first one is done for you.

bungalow	Hindustani – leg clothing
dandelion	Spanish – a courtyard
dinghy	Italian – little strings
ketchup	Italian – little worms
khaki	Urdu + Persian – dusty
patio	Hindi – a small boat
pyjamas	Old English – a spinner
robot	French – lion's teeth
spaghetti	Hindi – Bengal thatched house
spider	Czech – compulsory labour
terminus	Hindi – robber, murderer
thug	Malay – fish sauce
vermicelli	Latin – end, limit

If you get stuck, your dictionary will help you.

ADJECTIVES

Adjectives are describing words. They help to make a description lively and detailed.

They describe nouns:

The man had guns.

Bit dull, eh? Look how much more interesting things are when you add adjectives.

The bad man had big guns.

And look how important adjectives can be.

The bad man had big broken guns.

They can describe pronouns, too.

TIME FOR SOME FUNKY WORK

Describe a friend

List five adjectives that describe your best friend.

Stamp out the evil intruder

Cross out the word in each line which is NOT an adjective.

1.	happy	tall	bed	miserable
2.	delicious	apple	green	early
3.	across	sad	young	lazy
4.	lonely	small	expensive	car
5.	empty	myself	sunny	rich

Add an adjective

Add ten adjectives that will make this description more interesting.

The wind was _____. The night was _____.

The children were _____ as they trudged along

the _____ path through the wood. They

wished they were at home,_____ and

_____ in front of a _____ fire.

We asked two famous people and Colin to add their choice of adjectives to show how much difference it can make.

Look ➡

ALL THE DIFFERENCE IN THE WORLD

Enid the Nice Aunty

The wind was **nice**. The night was **warm**.
The children were **happy** and **cosy** as they trudged along the
lovely and **nice** path through the **pretty** wood. They wished they
were at home, **nice** and **happy** in front of a **pretty**, **cosy** fire.
And soon they were!

Mike the Horror Writer

The wind was **scary**. The night was **icy** and **cold**.
The children were **barefoot**, **tired**, **hungry**, **miserable**,
diseased and going **green** as they trudged along the **evil** path
through the **haunted** wood. They wished they were at home,
safe and **uninjured** in front of a **real** fire. Instead of fires of
Hell, which now awaited.

Yes, all right Mike, steady on.

Colin

The wind was **light** to **steady**. The night was **normal**.
The children were **normal** as they trudged along the **straight**
path through the **wooded** wood. They wished they were at home
average and **normal** in front of a **guarded** fire. The End.

FIVE KINDS OF ADJECTIVES

ADJECTIVES OF QUALITY

All the adjectives we've used so far have been adjectives of quality.
They're fun to use because they add vivid and interesting details.
Look at this dull sentence:

The dog has teeth.

Now add some adjectives of quality telling us what the teeth are like:

The dog has **huge yellow** <u>teeth</u>.

Use adjectives when you write to make your descriptions come to life.

DEMONSTRATIVE ADJECTIVES:

this   that   these   those

Demonstrative adjectives are "pointing out" adjectives:
that <u>bus</u>, **those** <u>computers</u>, **this** <u>book</u>, **these** <u>pens</u>.

That <u>dog</u> has yellow teeth.

Look at **those** <u>teeth</u>.

Can you see now why it is ungrammatical to say "them teeth"?

Them is a pronoun.

Colin is right. You need the demonstrative adjective "those", not the
personal pronoun "them".

Pronouns can't describe nouns.

ADJECTIVES OF QUANTITY

All the numbers (**one, two, three** ... and **first, second, third** ...)
are adjectives when they are used to describe nouns and pronouns.

These adjectives can add precise useful detail too.

The dog has **fifteen** huge yellow <u>teeth</u>.
The **first** <u>time</u> I saw them I was terrified.

Always write numbers as words when they are being used as adjectives.

SPELLING QUIZ

Write these numbers as words:

15 _____   40 _____

90 _____   5th _____

8th _____   12th _____

Check your answers at the back of the book – how did you do,
and what does it say about you?

7 or more: You are a liar and a cheat. There are only
6 questions.

6: Top marks – congratulations! Give yourself a chocolate and a
pat on the head, allow yourself to be carried around shoulder high
and pestered by autograph hunters for a bit... then carry on.

4-5: Pretty good; you're OK, you know? Just check those you got
wrong, then move on.

1-3: Oops! Don't be too hard on yourself, though. Don't forget
even... (insert the name of your favourite person here) ..... couldn't
spell these words at one stage in his/her life. Go through them till
you get them right, then go on.

0: Bad luck, Steven.

POSSESSIVE ADJECTIVES:

my   your   his   her   its   our   their

Possessive adjectives show ownership.

My <u>dog</u> is a bit bossy.

Other dogs wag **their** tails. My dog wags **its** finger at me.

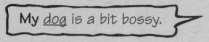

Notice that you DON'T need any apostrophes.

its – possessive adjective
it's – short form of it is / it has

INTERROGATIVE ADJECTIVES

These adjectives can begin questions by describing a noun.

Whose <u>dog</u> is this?

Colin's — don't you pay attention to anything?

What <u>subject</u> do you like best?

Which <u>film</u> did you see?

Which film?

Witch film

OUR NEW COMPETITION: SPOT THE SPOTS

SPOT THE DIFFERENCE:

whose – interrogative adjective
who's – short form of <u>who</u> <u>is</u> / <u>who</u> <u>has</u>

SPOT TEST:

1. _____ been eating my porridge?

2. _____ bicycle is that?

3. _____ mother can play the trumpet?

4. _____ coming to your party?

5. _____ penfriend lives in Germany?

SPOT CHECK:
its and it's

1. The butterfly spread _____ wings.

2. My cup has lost _____ handle.

3. _____ a lovely day today.

4. Smell that rose. _____ scent is wonderful.

5. _____ taken the five hours to find you.

SPOT THE DOG:

It's me again!

47

COMPARISON OF ADJECTIVES

BIG BIGGER BIGGEST

Add **-er** and **-est** to short adjectives to make comparisons.

Zelda is **tall** for her age. (positive)
Colin is **taller** than Zelda. (comparative)
Steven is **tallest** of all. (superlative)

ATTENTION!

Notice the spelling changes in some of these words.

short	shorter	shortest
sad	sadder	saddest
brave	braver	bravest
heavy	heavier	heaviest

Use **more** and **most** with longer adjectives

difficult	more difficult	most difficult
mysterious	more mysterious	most mysterious
intelligent	more intelligent	most intelligent
loving	more loving	most loving

Use **less** and **least** to go in the other direction.

difficult	less difficult	least difficult
mysterious	less mysterious	least mysterious
intelligent	less intelligent	least intelligent
loving	less loving	least loving

Remember these peculiar ones:
good better best
bad worse worst

YES
Now you can get your words in three different strengths!
NEW NEWER NEWEST formula

REMEMBER

- Use the comparative when you are comparing TWO people or things.

Zelda is **more beautiful** than Colin.
Zelda is **smaller** than Colin.

- Use the superlative when you are comparing THREE or more.

Zelda is the **most beautiful** of all.
Zelda is the **smallest**.

AND REMEMBER:

Never muddle up the two ways of forming the comparative.

Never muddle up the two ways of forming the superlative.

Steven is the most kindest monster I have ever met.   ✗
Apples are more nicer than pears.   ✗
Zelda is more beautifuller than you.   ✗
Steven is the kindest monster I have ever met.   ✓
Apples are nicer than pears.   ✓
Zelda is more beautiful than you.   ✓

And so:

Good man   **Comparatively Better Man**   **SUPERLATIVEMAN**

DID YOU KNOW?

Did you know that proper nouns are sometimes used as adjectives to describe other nouns?

A **London** <u>park</u>
A **Paris** <u>street</u>

Did you know that some adjectives have been made from proper nouns and still keep their capital letters?

An **English** <u>accent</u>
A **German** <u>car</u>

Did you know that common nouns are sometimes used as adjectives?

A **glass** <u>bottle</u>
A **grass** <u>skirt</u>
A **garden** <u>gnome</u>

Did you know that a group of words can do the work of an adjective?

A **happy-go-lucky** <u>smile</u>
A **don't-disturb-me-now** <u>frown</u>
Up-to-the-minute <u>styles</u>

Give me your <u>butter-wouldn't-melt-in-my-mouth</u> smile!

You are not just stupid. You are not just more stupid than other things like rocks and stones. You are the stupidest thing since Mr Stupid did a stupid thing stupidly.

COLIN'S CHALKBOARD CONCLUSIONS

ADJECTIVES

1. Adjectives describe nouns and pronouns.
2. When numbers are used as adjectives, always write them as words.
3. Don't say: look at them teeth. You need an adjective, not a pronoun.
   ✓ Look at those teeth.
4. Possessive adjectives don't need apostrophes.
5. Use the comparative form when comparing two things.
6. Use the superlative form when comparing three things or more.

Dynamic
Useful
Lovely
Likeable

Which of these words do you think best describes me?

That one.

DULL

51

JUST MESSING ABOUT

AMERICANISMS

If an American friend offers you a bag of chips, might they come wrapped in newspaper? No, definitely not! Americans call them chips, but we call them crisps.

If your friend offered you candy, what would you expect? Yes, sweets.

How many of these Americanisms can you "translate" into British English? You'll find the answers in the back of the book if you get stuck on any.

American English

1. cookies
2. checkers
3. comforter
4. crosswalk
5. deck (of cards)
6. diaper
7. elevator
8. the fall
9. faucet
10. fender (of a car)
11. garbage can
12. gas
13. hood (of a car)
14. overpass
15. pacifier
16. pants
17. purse
18. sidewalk
19. stroller
20. trunk (of a car)

British English

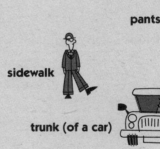
fender

pants

sidewalk

trunk (of a car)

checkers

deck (of cards)

the fall

VERBS

Verbs are DOING words and also BEING words.

DOING WORDS

Colin **saves** the ball.

Colin **swam** all the way to France.

Colin **drives** very fast and fantastically.

BEING WORDS

Colin **is** a big fibber about all of those things.

Colin **feels** a bit stupid now I've told you.

Their son **grew** very tall.

THE PRESENT TENSES

Verbs can show things happening in the past, in the present and in the future.

If you want to describe something happening NOW, you have three present tenses to choose from.

> I **shout** at Zelda.
>
> I **am shouting** at Zelda.
>
> I **do shout** at Zelda.

They each mean something very slightly different. You have to choose the one that fits your meaning best.

The first example means that I shout at Zelda and then stop.

The second example means that I am in the middle of shouting at Zelda.

The third example is a confession that I shout at poor Zelda rather a lot!

If you want to ask a question, you have to use the last two tenses.

Am I shouting at Zelda?

Do I shout at Zelda?

If you want to give
an order, you have
to use the first
and the last.

Do shut up!

Shout at Zelda!

Do shout at Zelda!

ROADSIDE CHECK

Circle the verbs in these sentences:

1. I hate cabbage and sprouts.
2. Steven punched Colin on the nose.
3. You are silly.
4. My dog eats vegetables.
5. We bought some fireworks.
6. Swallow your medicine.

Now let's have a bit of a rest before we talk about past tenses.

Did you know that some words can be used as nouns (naming words) and verbs (doing and being words)?
Here is an example: **shout**

Give a loud **shout**. (noun)
Shout loudly. (verb)

Oh don't start shouting again!

TEST YOUR UNDERSTANDING

Make up two sentences for each word (write your answers on a separate sheet of paper).
In the first sentence, use the word as a noun.
In the second sentence, use the word as a verb.

1.	kiss	4.	dream
2.	work	5.	walk
3.	help		

DICTIONARY WORK

Use your dictionary to help you make these nouns and adjectives into verbs by adding these endings: -ate, -en, -ify, -ise.
e.g. fertile + ise = fertilise

wide _____   pure _____   special _____

beauty _____   fabric _____

THE PAST TENSES

If you want to describe something that happened earlier today, or yesterday, or a long time ago, you need to use one of the past tenses. Use a past tense if something is now finished, over and done with.

I **shouted** at Zelda but she took no notice.
I **did shout** at Zelda, I admit, but I won't do it again.
I **have shouted** at Zelda all day and I have a headache now.
I **had shouted** at Zelda before I realised.
I **used to shout** at Zelda but I don't now.
I **was shouting** at Zelda when you arrived.

Yeah, that was a really good day.

Each past tense means something slightly different.

YOUR SHOUT

Use the past tense of <u>shout</u> that works best in these gaps.

1. I _____ at Zelda when the postman came but I stopped as soon as I saw him.

2. I _____ at Zelda when I was much younger but I don't now.

3. I _____ at Zelda when I saw the mess she had made.

4. I _____ at Zelda only once in my life.

Usually you add -ed and -ing to a verb to help form the past tenses, but some can be very peculiar.

Look at these:
to swim

I **swam** in the pool.
I **was swimming** in the pool.
I **have swum** in the pool.

to begin

I **began** my homework.
I **was beginning** my homework.
I **have begun** my homework.

to do

I **did** my homework.
I **was doing** my homework.
I **have done** my homework.

Your dictionary will always help you with verbs that don't follow the usual pattern. Look up what is called the infinitive (to _____). The infinitives of the examples above are given on the left: to swim, to begin, to do.

RIGHT OR WRONG

Put a cross beside Steven's mistakes.
Tick any of the tenses he's got right.

1. Colin seen it.
2. I done it.
3. Zelda catched it.
4. We have selled it.
5. You taked it.

DO IT YOURSELF

Fill the gaps with the right part of the verb. (The infinitive is in brackets at the end.)

1. The baby has _____ up. (to wake)
2. Nobody _____ to me yesterday. (to speak)
3. The water pipes have _____ . (to freeze)
4. We all _____ to understand but we couldn't. (to try)
5. I _____ you had gone home. (to think)

THE FUTURE TENSES

Anything happening in a minute, or later today, or tomorrow, or after that will be in one of the future tenses.

Will you avoid shouting, this time, please?

There are several of them and there are slight differences in meaning.

I **shall ask** Zelda.
I **will ask** Zelda.

I **shall be asking** Zelda.
I **will be asking** Zelda.

I **am going to ask** Zelda.
I **am about to ask** Zelda.

Look at the last two examples. In both examples, I clearly plan to ask Zelda something but I'm closer to actually doing it in the second sentence.

I am about to ask Zelda. (= very soon now!)

Look at the middle two examples. In both sentences, Zelda is clearly going to be asked something in the future but in the second sentence there is more determination!

I shall be asking Zelda. (when I get a chance)
I will be asking Zelda. (whatever happens)

Similarly, with the first two examples. The first sentence suggests that Zelda will be asked in the normal course of events. The second sentence means that I fully intend to ask Zelda whatever it is that's on my mind!

Go on then. I'm listening!

Will it be OK if I do some more shouting?

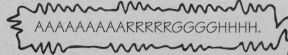

AAAAAAAAAARRRRRGGGGHHHH.

Notice how you can switch from simple future tense to a future tense full of determination and will-power.

Look carefully at **shall** and **will**.

SIMPLE FUTURE

Singular	Plural
I **shall** ask	we **shall** ask
you **will** ask	you **will** ask
he/she/it **will** ask	they **will** ask

FUTURE WITH DETERMINATION ADDED

I **will** ask	we **will** ask
you **shall** ask	you **shall** ask
he/she/it **shall** ask	they **shall** ask

I WILL dance with you!

I **will** die first!

You **SHALL** go to the teashop for a light snack!

I was sort of hoping for a ball, really.

Most people don't bother about the subtle difference in meaning between *shall* and *will* and possibly in time we shall all forget about it. That is how language develops. At the moment, however, the difference exists and it's worth taking care over.

And now an example of the tenses you've seen, in exciting action.

YOUR CUT OUT 'N' KEEP TROUSER SOUVENIR.
THE AMAZING MR TROUSERS USES ALL THE TENSES IN ONE GO.

Is it a bird? Is it a plane? No... it's Mr Trousers...
Right here goes then... everybody ready? Right... "I used to wear short trousers, but in 1970 my legs got hairy, so until 1995 I wore long, baggy trousers. Now I wear long non-baggy trousers. One day, I shall wear no trousers at all. That'll make people take notice."
Cheer now! Accept no substitute.

Mr Trousers — original and best.

AUXILIARY VERBS

Otherwise known as HELPING verbs.

Verbs that help other verbs to make tenses are called auxiliary (or helping) verbs.

The most common auxiliary verbs are:

to be   **to have**   **to do**

I **did** enjoy your book.
I **have** devoured every page.
I **have been** chewing them.

The slide show of my interesting gravel collection **will be** showing tonight. I **am** hoping you will come.

I'm sorry, I **will be** washing my hair.

Zelda **had been** dirtying it all day so that she **would** have an excuse.

Underline the auxiliary verbs in these sentences and put a box around the main verbs.

1. You do look nice.
2. Cinderella, you shall go to the ball.
3. I have forgotten your name.
4. My father was snoring very loudly.
5. He is learning French.

Add suitable auxiliary verbs in the spaces.

6. They _____ collecting firewood.
7. My neighbour _____ won £10,000.
8. Everybody _____ cheering very loudly at yesterday's match.
9. We _____ hear the results tomorrow.
10. I _____ not know the answer.

MORE AUXILIARY VERBS

might   must   could   would   should

These auxiliary verbs cause no trouble used like this:

I **might** <u>tell</u>.
I **must** <u>tell</u>.
I **could** <u>tell</u>.
I **would** <u>tell</u>.
I **should** <u>tell</u>.

I **William Tell**.

But some people CAN'T HANDLE them in constructions like these:

I **might** of <u>told</u>. ✗
I **must** of <u>told</u>. ✗
I **could** of <u>told</u>. ✗
I **would** of <u>told</u>. ✗
I **should** of <u>told</u>. ✗

I **might** have <u>told</u>. ✓
I **must** have <u>told</u>. ✓
I **could** have <u>told</u>. ✓
I **would** have <u>told</u>. ✓
I **should** have <u>told</u>. ✓

If you want to shorten these constructions you can do it like this:

I might've told.
I must've told.
I could've told.
I would've told.
I should've told.

But don't make the SILLY mistake of thinking that **must've** is written **must of**!!

Who would of thought it!

You *could've* – *should've* – used **would've**.

61

CONTRACTIONS

Otherwise known as shortened forms!

While we're talking about contractions like could've, let's revise a few more.

 There are TWO in that last sentence!

 I mean you're ... it's ... isn't it? ooh, He'd... I'm er not sure about.. I'll... I'll...

Here are just a few:

I'll = I will	I'll phone you tomorrow.
I'll = I shall	I'll be ten years old tomorrow.
you've = you have	You've got very big eyes.
he'd = he had	He'd lost all his money.
he'd = he would	He'd have preferred to go to Spain.
we're = we are	We're sorry about that.
it's = it is	It's not fair.
it's = it has	It's been a lovely day.
can't = cannot	I can't hear you.
isn't = is not	It isn't fair.

NORMAL SIZE

Here's a brain.   **It's contracted.**   **It's tiny.**

Isn't that Steven's?

 So that's where I left it.

WIN A TROPHY NOW!*

Put apostrophes where they're needed.
Some sentences DON'T need any!

1. If I have any more to eat Ill feel ill.
2. Its quite true that the cat chases its tail every evening.
3. I cant believe thats true.
4. Were sorry we werent there.
5. My chewing gum has lost its flavour.
6. Didnt you know that theyd moved?
7. Where were you yesterday?
8. Youre always moaning about your teachers.
9. I mustve told you who they are.
10. Your rabbit has broken its hutch.

If you get 9/10 or more, award yourself this:

THE APOS TROPHY

I am not stupid

---

* *This time it is true – hooray!*

THE INFINITIVE

We've talked about infinitives already. They're the basic form of the verb, usually beginning with to.

To Infinitive, And Beyond!

Here are some examples:

I tried **to ride** a camel in Egypt.
I hope **to go** to university.
They let me help them (**to**) **paint** the house.

When people talk about SPLIT INFINITIVES, they mean a word has been put in the middle of an infinitive.

My father started **to** noisily **snore**.
He decided **to** never **wash** again.

Usually there's no point in splitting an infinitive because the sentence would sound better if you didn't.

My father started to snore noisily. ✓
He decided never to wash again. ✓

BUT if you think your sentence would sound better IF YOU DID SPLIT the infinitive, then go ahead. It's NOT a crime. You're free to do it.

Are you advising them to *deliberately on certain occasions when they feel like it* split their infinitives? MONSTROUS!

Monstrous? Even I can tell he's split his infinitive all right!

THE SPLIT INFINITIVE SPECIAL EDITION FOR PEOPLE WITH TIME TO SLOWLY PASS

One of the most famous split infinitives of all time, including the future, is of course featured at the beginning of *Star Trek*.

To baldly go where no man has gone before.

Star Trek shows the way ahead. Not that we're all about to start wearing those tight-fitting sweatshirts and black trousers, but the split infinitive is becoming more and more acceptable.

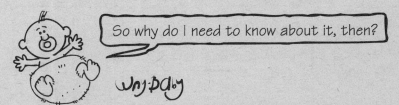

So why do I need to know about it, then?

Why Baby

Well, you should be aware that sometimes it sounds better not to split the infinitive, like in the examples opposite.

Perhaps more importantly, however, you can feel a little smug every time someone splits an infinitive badly.

THE PRESENT PARTICIPLE

PRESENT PARTICIPLE

Just what I was hoping to get – a present participle.

PAST PARTICIPLE

So much better than the past participle.

Present participles always end in **-ing**. They do TWO jobs:

1)   They help to form tenses.
       Colin is **mowing** the lawn today.
       Colin was **mowing** the lawn yesterday.
       Colin will be **mowing** the lawn tomorrow.
2)   They describe nouns and pronouns.
       <u>Colin</u> hurt his toe, **mowing** the lawn.
       <u>She</u> sat in the chair, **trembling** all over.

THE PAST PARTICIPLE

Past participles usually end in -ed but there are some exceptions.

To find the past participle, take a verb and complete the phrase:
having been . . .

to carry	having been	⟶	**carried**
to watch	having been	⟶	**watched**
to finish	having been	⟶	**finished**
to choose	having been	⟶	**chosen**
to buy	having been	⟶	**bought**
to see	having been	⟶	**seen**

Past participles can do TWO jobs too.

1) They help form tenses.
   The present was **chosen** with great care.
   Colin has **mown** the lawn.
2) They describe nouns and pronouns.
   Exhausted by his efforts, <u>Colin</u> rested.
   Watched by thousands, <u>he</u> crossed the line.

Be careful when you're using participles to describe nouns and pronouns. If you're not careful, they can describe the wrong ones.

Why is this sentence ridiculous?

MOWING THE LAWN, A STONE HIT COLIN ON THE NOSE.

It's ridiculous because it sounds as if it was THE STONE that was MOWING the lawn.

As we happen to know that it was Colin, we could rewrite the sentence in two ways to make it clear:

Mowing the lawn, Colin was hit on the nose by a stone.
While he was mowing the lawn, Colin was hit on the nose by a stone.

Always make sure that the participle relates to the right noun or to the right pronoun. Be on the look-out for any possible misunderstandings.

SPANNERS AT THE READY; IT'S REPAIR TIME

Can you rewrite these misleading sentences?

1. Walking round the corner,
   my cottage is on the left.

_____

2. Skipping happily across the road,
   a bicycle nearly knocked her over.

_____

3. Well known for ill-health and muggings,
   Mary Poppins lived in the London of the 1890s.

_____

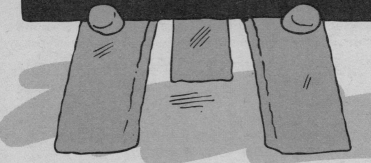

COLIN'S CHALKBOARD CONCLUSIONS

VERBS

1. Verbs are doing and being words.
2. Auxiliary verbs help to make tenses.
3. Dictionaries help with irregular spellings.
4. There are no such constructions as:
   might of – must of – could of –
   would of – should of
   might have ✓ might've ✓.
5. Contractions need apostrophes.
6. Make sure participles describe the right noun or pronoun.

COLIN'S MISLEADING ADVICE NO. 14.

Parti-ciples are like disciples – except they go to more parties. Because they always bring a present, "present" participles go to lots. "Past" parti-ciples tend to go on about how they used to be better, whereas Disco-ciples only go to...

ADVERBS

Adverbs mostly describe verbs. They add important information. They tell us HOW, WHEN and WHERE things are done.

ADVERBS OF MANNER TELL US HOW SOMETHING IS DONE.

Colin droned on **endlessly**. My mother smiled **gently**. Steven tries **hard**.

ADVERBS OF TIME TELL US WHEN SOMETHING IS DONE.

The doctor came **immediately**.   We all laughed **afterwards**. I will always be **grateful**.

ADVERBS OF PLACE TELL US WHERE SOMETHING IS DONE.

I left the money **there**. We looked **everywhere**. Gather **round**.

ADVERBS OF DEGREE are a little different because they describe other adverbs and adjectives.

My parents were **very** angry.
They were **extremely** cross.
They shouted **really** loudly.

"THE ADVERB FAMILY GOES COMPLETELY MAD"

THRILL as the family fights for its right to describe verbs –
accurately, repeatedly, fairly and often!
GASP as they swing into action, here, now, above you,
behind you, and everywhere!
CRY as they are used too frequently, badly, painfully, inappropriately.
SAY "THIS IS QUITE A LAUGH THEN" as the family runs
about idiotically, clumsily, and hilariously awkwardly!
STOP – suddenly.

In order to liven up these exercises, we're going to do them whilst doing a line dance, OK? Everybody ready?
Take your partner by the hand and
Add an adverb where you stand.

1. The twins whispered _____ .

2. We made our beds _____ .

3. I ate the apple pie _____ .

4. We are _____ sorry for what we did.

5. Zelda tied the parcel _____ .

Bend over now y'all by the knees.
Make an adverb, er... if you please.
Careful y'all with the spelling
Otherwise, there's no telling (what will happen)

6. safe _____

7. careful _____

8. merry _____

9. sincere _____

10. real _____

Chicken in a basket, pickin' up sticks
See if you know the opposites (to these words).

11. seldom _____

12. most _____

13. quickly _____

14. always _____

15. loosely _____

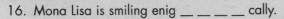

Swing your elders, swing your betters
See if you can tell the missing letters
Listen now and pay good heed,
Use a dictionary if you need.

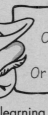

16. Mona Lisa is smiling enig __ __ __ __ cally.

17. Steven is smiling stu __ idly.

Dosey-do and eat the cake.
Can you pick out each mistake?
If you can, now put it right
Or else with me you'll have to fight.

18. I am learning to type proper.

19. Everyone is behaving really strange.

20. Zelda plays the flute beautiful.

21. He spoke rather fierce.

Now it's time to stop our prancing
And time for me to give up line dancing.
I really want to be a lumberjack.

SAY WHAT YOU MEAN

Be very careful when you use the adverbs HARDLY and SCARCELY.

If you use NOT in the same sentence, you could end up saying the very opposite of what you mean.

For example:

Colin's <u>not</u> wearing <u>hardly</u> any clothes.   *means*

Colin's wearing a lot of clothes.

If you mean to describe this awful sight . . .

then you should say:

Colin is wearing **hardly** any clothes.

BE VERY CAREFUL AGAIN

Take care when you use the word ONLY. It really does matter where you put it in a sentence. It will describe the nearest word.

Only <u>Zelda</u> can buy sweets on Fridays.
(= nobody else)

Zelda can buy **only** <u>sweets</u> on Fridays.
(= nothing else)

Zelda can buy sweets **only** <u>on Fridays</u>.
(= at no other time)

COMPARISON OF ADVERBS

Steven dives **gracefully**.

Colin dives **more gracefully**.

Zelda dives **most gracefully**.

Add **-er** and **-est** to short adverbs to make comparisons.

Steven works **hard**. (positive)
Colin works **harder**. (comparative)
Zelda works the **hardest**. (superlative)

Use **more** and **most** with other adverbs.

calmly	more calmly	most calmly
kindly	more kindly	most kindly
carelessly	more carelessly	most carelessly
energetically	more energetically	most energetically

Use **less** and **least** to go in the other direction.

energetically	less energetically	least energetically

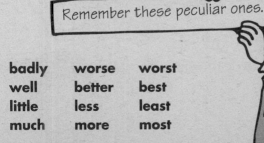

Remember these peculiar ones.

badly	**worse**	**worst**
well	**better**	**best**
little	**less**	**least**
much	**more**	**most**

Adjectives and adverbs together: The Hardest Test Known Ever, Brought Exclusively To You.

Start at number 1. See if you can say the answer out loud. If, when you move on to the square mentioned, you discover you got it right, answer the next question, and so on. When you get one wrong, go back to the start.

1 What is the comparative of the adverb "hard"? Go forward to 5.	**2** *Most softly.* What's the comparative of "softly"? Go to 13.	**3** *Adverb – comparative of late.* What's the superlative of "many"? Go to 9.	**4** *Most tunefully.* What's the superlative of "near"? Go to 8.
8 *Nearest.* What part of speech is "later"? Go to 3.	**7** *Less.* What's the superlative of "softly"? Go to 2.	**6** *Adverb – superlative.* What's the superlative of "good"? Go to 10.	**5** *Harder.* What's the superlative of the adjective "easy"? Go to 12.
9 *Most.* What's the superlative of "badly"? Go forward to 14.	**10** *Best.* What's the superlative of "tunefully"? Go to 4.	**11** *Best.* What part of speech is "most clumsily"? Go to 6.	**12** *Easiest.* What's the comparative of the adverb "quietly"? Go to 15.
16 FINISHED! Tremendously well done. Most tremendously well done, in fact.	**15** *More quietly.* What's the superlative of "well"? Go to 11.	**14** *Worst.* What's the comparative of "little"? Go to 7.	**13** *More softly.* Go to 16.

COLIN'S CHALKBOARD CONCLUSIONS

ADVERBS

1. Adverbs describe verbs and other adverbs.

2. **Scarcely** and **hardly** are negatives.

3. Be careful to put **only** in front of the right word.

4. In comparisons, we use -**er** and -**est** with short adverbs; **more** and **most** with the others.

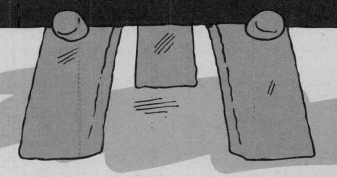

When you've 'ad enough of verbs by themselves, just 'add an adverb!

His attempts at humour are quickly, sadly, tragically getting worse.

JUST MESSING ABOUT

Some slang expressions have entered the language from the East End of London from Cockney rhyming slang.

You'll know some of them:

plates of <u>meat</u>	feet
trouble and <u>strife</u>	wife
apples and <u>pears</u>	stairs

Some expressions are not so straightforward because the rhyming word is left out!

use your loaf   (loaf of <u>bread</u>)   use your head

me ol' China   (china <u>plate</u>)   mate

Here are some more Cockney rhyming slang phrases.

chew the <u>fat</u>	have a chat
not a dickey-<u>bird</u>	not a word
mince <u>pies</u>	eyes
daisy <u>roots</u>	boots
Cain & <u>Abel</u>	table
skin and <u>blister</u>	sister
God <u>forbids</u>	kids
Hampstead <u>Heath</u>	teeth
North & <u>South</u>	mouth
dog and <u>bone</u>	phone
raspberry <u>(tart)</u>	heart
Oliver <u>(Twist)</u>	fist
titfer (tit for <u>tat</u>)	hat
bread (and <u>honey</u>)	money
porkies (pork <u>pies</u>)	lies

After I hurt me plates, I was talking to my skin and blister on the dog and bone with me raspberry in my daisies, straight up.

What!?

PREPOSITIONS

Prepositions are little words like

on   by   from   for   with   to   of   in   at

You'll see from these examples the important job they do in sentences. They show connections.

<u>My cat</u> is hiding **under** <u>the bed</u>.

<u>Your coat</u> is **on** <u>the floor</u>.

<u>This poem</u> is **by** <u>Roald Dahl</u>.

Here is a <u>message</u> **from** <u>the Queen</u>.

Give <u>that</u> **to** <u>me</u>.

SHIP IN A BOTTLE

Notice that in the last example, the pronoun form is **me** not I.

Use me, you, him, her, us, them after prepositions.

This <u>invitation</u> is **for** <u>you</u>.
This <u>invitation</u> is **for** <u>me</u>.
This <u>invitation</u> is **for** <u>you and me</u>.
This <u>invitation</u> is **for** <u>us</u>.

This chocolate is for us.   **This chocolate is for me.**

SPOT THE DIFFERENCE

What's the difference in meaning in each pair?

1.   drop in

      drop out

2.   laugh at

      laugh off

3.   give away

      give up

DON'T BE PREPOSTEROUS

PREPOSTEROUS REX (EXTINCT)

Choose the right preposition.

Your dictionary will help you.

1. They're always complaining _____ us.

2. We're hoping _____ good results.

3. I prefer chocolate _____ sweets.

4. She agrees _____ everything you say.

5. My uncle has given _____ smoking.

CAN YOU END A SENTENCE WITH A PREPOSITION?

Some people say that you never should. Others say that it all depends on whether the sentence sounds better with a preposition at the end or somewhere else.

Generally speaking, most sentences sound better if they don't end with a preposition. Compare these two questions:

Can you use a preposition to end a sentence **with**?
Can you end a sentence **with** a preposition?

However, there are other cases where the sentence sounds really peculiar if you try to avoid having the preposition at the end:

What are you waiting **for**?
For what are you waiting?

Make up your own mind. Try the sentence both ways and then decide.

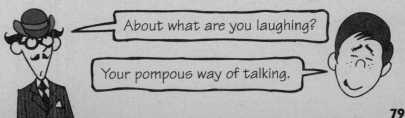

About what are you laughing?

Your pompous way of talking.

COLIN'S CHALKBOARD CONCLUSIONS

PREPOSITIONS

1. Prepositions are little words that connect.

2. Use the right preposition. Your dictionary will help you.

3. End a sentence with a preposition if it sounds better that way.

So this man, right, comes up to me and says, right, that he can prove that his favourite parts of speech are the little fleshy bits of the fruit with a stone in it, away from the furry skin. So I say to him... "That's a ridiculous preposition!" Get it? A ridiculous — not proposition, but "preposition"!

Does it occur to you he might have been talking about "parts of peach"?

Ah, no.

Nurse! Nurse! Colin's out of bed again.

CONJUNCTIONS AND INTERJECTIONS

Conjunctions JOIN.

ANDCUFFS.

COORDINATING CONJUNCTIONS

and   but   or

These join two of the same kind and keep them equally important.

fish **and** chips
slowly **but** surely
sink **or** swim

Make sure you always choose the one you need. They each have a different meaning and some people don't realise that.

and   but   or

Use each just once in the right place.

1. He is tired _____ he won't stop.

2. Do you like maths _____ English best?

3. Holidays are fun _____ I always look forward to them.

Now use them all in one sentence:

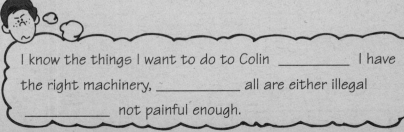

I know the things I want to do to Colin _____ I have
the right machinery, _____ all are either illegal
_____ not painful enough.

CORRELATIVE CONJUNCTIONS

not only . . . but also
both . . . and
either . . . or
neither . . . nor

He's **not only** handsome **but also** intelligent.
His mother was **both** amazed **and** delighted.
You are **either** mad **or** thinking of someone else.
I have **neither** forgotten **nor** forgiven the time he sat gnawing a
bone for an hour. When he stood up his leg fell off.

> You do have to be **both**
> very sensible **and** very careful!

It's true you have to be careful where you put
each half of the pair to keep the sentence balanced.

My mother either told me to tidy my
room or to take the dog for a walk. **✗**

My mother told me   1) to tidy my room
                     2) to take the dog for a walk

My mother told me **either** to tidy
my room **or** to take the dog for a walk. **✓**

PUT THIS SENTENCE RIGHT

Steven not only is lazy but also greedy.

> Steven is fab?

No. I mean put it right grammatically.

SUBORDINATING CONJUNCTIONS

These join by making one statement follow on from another in a dependent way.

WHY?

She did well **because** she worked hard.

WHEN?

Zelda will contact you **when** the spare part comes.

HOW?

He looked **as though** he'd seen a ghost.

WHY?

I gave her a lift **because** she was late.

Here are some subordinating conjunctions:

after	**if***	**until**
although	**in order that**	**when**
as	**since**	**whenever**
as if	**so . . . that**	**where**
as though	**so that**	**wherever**
because	**that**	**whether***
before	**though**	**while**
for	**unless**	**whilst**

*__if__ and **whether** are alternatives.

You must finish the sentence... and make it funny!

1. Wait here until _____ .
2. He cleared his throat before _____ .
3. I'll buy the bicycle if _____ .
4. Tracey enjoyed the book because _____ .
5. My father doubled my pocket money, although _____ .

Pick a conjunction – any conjunction.

6. Debbie can dance _____ she's playing the violin.
7. I tripped over the mat _____ I came in.
8. He doesn't know _____ he'll be in London.
9. We like Zelda _____ she's very kind.
10. My dog follows me _____ I go.

INTERJECTIONS

When you hurt your toe and say "**Ouch!**", you are using an interjection.

When you jump in the air and say "**Yippee!**", you are using an interjection.

Interjections are short exclamations that express feelings.

Here are some that express pain, delight, joy, relief, shock, horror, disgust and fear.

CAPTAIN INTERJECTION

DOCTOR INJECTION

Ow! Ouch! Yippee! Hooray!
Gosh! Wow! Phew! Ah! Oh!
Oh dear! Aaargh! Bah! Help!
Ugh! Boo! Oops! Pshaw!

Interjections can be written as separate sentences of their own or they can be written as separate parts at the beginning of longer sentences.

OI! YOU! NOW!

Write a sentence that fits the interjection.

1. Ouch!

2. Yippee!

3. Gosh!

4. Ugh!

5. Wow!

How about "Yippee! I'm a hippy!"?

COLIN'S CHALKBOARD CONCLUSIONS

CONJUNCTIONS AND INTERJECTIONS

1. Conjunctions join.

2. Use the right conjunction.

3. Correlative conjunctions are used in pairs. Put each half of the pair in the right place.

4. Interjections are short exclamations.

5. Interjections can be used on their own or at the beginning of sentences.

JUST MESSING ABOUT

All the abbreviations below are abbreviations of Latin words.
Do you know the Latin words they stand for?

A.D.	anno domini	in the year of the Lord
a.m.	ante meridiem	before noon
cf.	confer	compare
C.V.	curriculum vitae	summary of career and life
D.V.	Deo volente	if God is willing
e.g.	exempli gratia	for example
etc.	et cetera	and the rest
i.e.	id est	that is
l.i.d.b	latinus ista deadus boringus	Latin is dead boring (not a real one)
N.B.	nota bene	note carefully
p.m.	post meridiem	after noon
P.S.	post scriptum	after the writing
R.I.P.	requiescat in pace	may he/she rest in peace
Q.E.D.	quid erat demonstrandum	which was to be shown or proved
v.	versus	against
viz	videlicit	namely

Is R.S.V.P. Latin?

No, it's from the French:
Répondez s'il vous plaît.
It means: please reply.

I don't think I'll bother!

Do you ever get muddled up when you use **e.g.** and **i.e.**?
Use **e.g.** when you are going to give an example.
Citrus fruits, **e.g.** lemons and oranges, are rich in Vitamin C.
Use **i.e.** when you are going to give an explanation or a
definition. All external examination candidates, **i.e.** those
taking GCSE and A-level examinations, should stay behind
after Assembly.

SENTENCES

Of all the parts of speech that we have studied, which is the one vital one in a sentence?

Well, yes. It's ONE of those but *WHICH ONE*?

Let's put the question another way.
Look at the three sentences below.
One is a statement, one is a question and one is a command.
What is the ONE part of speech they have in common?

> We ate three doughnuts each.
> Are you interested?
> Look!

Each sentence has a . . .

A verb.

Each sentence has a verb and it's a very special kind of verb.

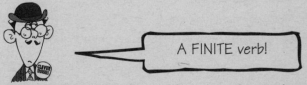

A FINITE verb!

Well done! Each sentence has a finite verb and you haven't learnt about these yet.

Turn to the next page and you'll learn about FINITE VERBS.

FINITE VERBS

Finite verbs have subjects.

Don't panic! Come back. We'll explain.

In the sentences below, we've put the subjects in boxes and underlined the verbs.

| Steven | is laughing.

| The grass | is being cut.

| Lollipops | make you sticky.

| We | have lost our way.

Put WHO or WHAT in front of the verbs and you'll find the subjects.

WHO is laughing?   Steven

WHAT is being cut?   The grass

WHAT make you sticky?   Lollipops

WHO have lost the way? We

All the sentences above are statements. Commands and questions have subjects too but they're not quite so easy to find. We'll look at commands first.

LOOK OUT!

WHO should look out? (It doesn't say but you jolly well know who's meant to look out if someone shouts at you!) YOU.

<u>Come</u> here!	You <u>come</u> here!
<u>Shut</u> up!	You <u>shut</u> up!
<u>Go</u> to bed!	You <u>go</u> to bed!

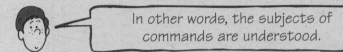

In other words, the subjects of commands are understood.

Yes. You can call them UNDERSTOOD, or IMPLIED, or TAKEN FOR GRANTED or LEFT OUT FOR THE SAKE OF BREVITY. But the verbs in commands are finite verbs. They could have their subjects there if they wanted.

Now let's look at questions. The word order in questions is a bit complicated as the subjects can come later than in statements.

<u>Is</u> **Steven** <u>laughing</u>?
<u>Is</u> **the grass** <u>being cut</u>?
<u>Do</u> **lollipops** <u>make</u> you sticky?
<u>Have</u> **we** <u>lost</u> our way?

OK?

So to sum up:

EVERY SENTENCE (WHETHER A COMMAND, A QUESTION, OR A STATEMENT) HAS TO HAVE A FINITE VERB.

Yes, it does.

He's got it, you know.

That's right.

He has, yes.

Now take a deep breath because we are going to spend half a page talking about non-finite verbs.

They sound complicated but they're not!

NON-FINITE VERBS

the infinitive
the present participle
the past participle

Do you remember these from the section on verbs?

to choose	infinitive
choosing	present participle
chosen	past participle

They're not finite verbs because they can't have subjects and so they can't be sentences on their own. Even if you wrote them out neatly with a capital letter at the beginning and a full stop at the end, they wouldn't be sentences.

They wouldn't be sentences because EVERY SENTENCE NEEDS A FINITE VERB and the infinitive, the present participle and the past participle are NOT finite verbs. They are only parts of verbs.

EVERY SENTENCE NEEDS A FINITE VERB.

He's still right.

Sure is.

He's got it, that boy.

Sure has.

FIND THE SENTENCES

There are three sentences hidden here.
Write them properly punctuated in the spaces at the end.

1. laughing all the way to the bank.

2. he was very cross

3. to cook a really delicious meal

4. chosen as partners

5. my mother gave me 50p

6. burnt to a cinder

7. coming round the corner without looking.

8. you must be joking

9. mowing the lawn before breakfast

10. reduced for a second time

_____

_____

_____

Elementary, my dear Watson.

A lemon entry?

JUST MESSING ABOUT TIME FOR WOULD-BE GENIUSES

Questions are written with a question mark at the end. Agreed?

> **"How are you?" he asked.**
> **"Would you like an ice cream?" she enquired.**

If you make these questions into reported statements, you won't need question marks or speech marks.

> **He asked me how I was.**
> **She asked if I would like an ice cream.**

Similarly, shouted commands are written with an exclamation mark at the end.

> **"Stand still, boy!" ordered the angry teacher.**
> **"Go to bed!" said my mother firmly.**

If you make these commands into reported statements, you won't need exclamation marks or speech marks.

> **The angry teacher ordered the boy to stand still.**
> **My mother told me firmly to go to bed.**

Stop, thief!

Why don't _you_ stop?

The policeman ordered the police to stop. The thief asked the policeman why he didn't stop instead.

A QUESTIONABLE COMMAND PERFORMANCE

Change these commands and questions into statements

1. "Blow your nose!" ordered my father.

    My father ordered me _____ .

2. "Get up!" my mother said to my sister.

    My mother told my sister_____ .

3. "Are you feeling better?" asked my teacher.

    My teacher asked me_____ .

4. "How much are the tomatoes?" the old lady asked the shopkeeper.

    The old lady asked the shopkeeper_____ .

5. "Will you tie my shoelaces?" my little brother asked.

    My little brother asked me _____ .

Toby or not Toby? That is the question.

The aggressively forgetful vicar checked with the parents whether their child's name was Toby.

IMPROVING YOUR SENTENCES

If you're happy with your written style, then this section is not so important for you – although *everybody* can improve.

If, on the other hand, you're not happy when you read through your work, if you know you've written in short jerky sentences but don't know what you can do about them, then you should find this section useful.

You'll find that you can experiment in all sorts of ways with combining short sentences into longer more complex ones. Remember, of course, that, used sparingly, short sentences can often be very effective. You really want a careful mixture of sentences of different lengths.

Be critical of your work. Don't be content with the first draft if you feel it can be improved. Be prepared to write several drafts of an important piece of work until it reads as well as you can make it.

Let's assume, for instance, that you've written this paragraph and are not happy with it:

> We all decided to go to Exmouth on Sunday. It was very hot. We were determined to swim. We all stayed in the water for a long time. We had each brought a packed lunch. We shared everything. We had a game of cricket on the sands. We all enjoyed that. It got rather cold in the middle of the afternoon. We decided to go home early. We'd had a really good time.

But that makes perfect sense...
Why can't I be happy with that?

Well...

Some people are bossy. They say keep them short. Fine. You can read them easily. That's good. For a bit. But not all the time. Eh? It starts getting irritating. Doesn't it? Like someone jabbing you. Going, "Hm?", "Hm?", "Hm?"...

Having said that, don't imagine for one moment that all your sentences should be long because that would be wrong for the simple reason that this sort of sentence eventually gets harder and harder to follow, quite apart from being

terribly dull.

So you might want to vary the length. That's why you need to know ways of joining.

Coordinating conjunctions: <u>and</u>, <u>but</u>, <u>or</u>

You don't want to rely solely on coordinating conjunctions. (You could end up with an awful rambling paragraph: we all decided to go to Exmouth on Sunday and it was very hot and we were . . .) However, one or two could certainly help our disjointed paragraph.

Perhaps:

It was very hot and we were determined to swim.

or:

We were determined to swim and we all stayed in the water for some time.

NOW you know why you shouldn't start a sentence with AND or BUT or OR. They are words for *joining* sentences and so will be somewhere in the middle of a sentence, not at the beginning.

SUBORDINATING CONJUNCTIONS

after	although	as	as if	as though	because
before	for	if	in order that	since	so . . . that
so that	that	though	unless	until	when
whenever	where	wherever	while	whilst	

Here are just a few of the possible combinations:

Sunday was **so** hot **that** we all decided to go to Exmouth.

As it got rather cold in the middle of the afternoon, we decided to go home early.

Although we went home early **because** it got cold in the middle of the afternoon, we'd had a really good time.

USING WHO, WHOM, WHOSE, WHICH, THAT

Use **who** and **whom** for people.

Use **which** and **that** for things.

Whose can refer to both people and things.

Zelda is the person **who** does all the work around here.

She is the person **whom** I admire most.

Either: We had each brought a packed lunch **which** we shared.

or: We had each brought a packed lunch **that** we shared.

Either: We had a game of cricket on the sands **which** we all enjoyed.

or: We had a game of cricket on the sands **that** we all enjoyed.

USING PARTICIPLES

Determined to swim, we all stayed in the water for a long time.

Having each **brought** a packed lunch, we shared everything.

After **sharing** the packed lunches each of us had brought, we had a game of cricket on the sands.

BEING MORE CONCISE

You may find that you can use just a few words to replace a whole sentence.

We had a game of cricket on the sands. We all enjoyed that.

= We all had an enjoyable game of cricket on the sands.

We had each brought a packed lunch. We shared everything.

= We shared our packed lunches.

No two people would rewrite the paragraph in exactly the same way. There are so many possibilities that no two people would choose exactly the same set in the same sequence.

Here is one possible second draft:

Sunday was so hot that we all decided to go to Exmouth. We were determined to swim and stayed in the water for a long time. After sharing our packed lunches, we had an enjoyable game of cricket on the sands. Although we went home early because it got cold in the middle of the afternoon, we'd had a really good time.

You might want to work further on this, tinkering and polishing, of course. Drafting and redrafting is a very important part of the creative process.

GET IT TOGETHER

Use any method you like to combine each of these groups of short sentences into single sentences.

1. Matt tidied his bedroom. He washed up the breakfast things. He had forgotten to buy a present. It was Mother's Day.

   _____

   _____

2. I have flu. I have all the usual symptoms. I have a sore throat. I have a high temperature. I don't feel like eating anything. I have no energy.

   _____

   _____

   _____

3. Sarah was nervous. It was her first day at her new school. She knew nobody. It was a huge building. "I shall get lost," she thought. She had a different teacher for every lesson. It was confusing at first.

   _____

   _____

   _____

   _____

SENTENCE BOUNDARIES

No, Steven. Not that kind of boundary.

Always take care to show where one sentence ends and another begins.

This may sound very simple but you'd be AMAZED at how many people don't use end stops (full stops, or question marks, or exclamation marks) at the ends of sentences. You don't want to be stupid like them, do you?

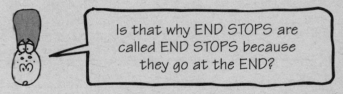

Is that why END STOPS are called END STOPS because they go at the END?

Yes, Steven, it is. What's more, ONLY end stops will do – you can't use commas instead. Commas can't do the special work of a full stop, a question mark, or an exclamation mark. Commas can't show where a sentence ends.

ROADSIDE CHECK

Circle the four places where full stops are needed instead of commas.

As a half-term treat, Steven, Colin and Zelda are going camping in the New Forest, fortunately they've been able to borrow a tent, a groundsheet and a camping-stove, they already have warm sleeping bags, all week, it seems, they have been making lists, buying last-minute items, and packing rucksacks, the weather forecast is not very good but they'll enjoy themselves whatever the weather, if I know them.

COLIN'S DIARY

Colin says that he'll put the end stops in when he gets home. Can you help by circling all the places where he needs a full stop, a question mark or an exclamation mark?

Friday 30 May

We managed to get the tent up Steven wasn't much help it's lucky that I know something about camping Zelda forgot to pack the mallet fortunately I thought of using a tin of baked beans to bang the tent pegs in with what would they do without me they've got no ideas of their own

Saturday 31 May

It rained all night luckily our sleeping bags are still dry it was Steven's turn to cook today we had a dreadful breakfast what will he be giving us tonight the New Forest ponies are very timid can you blame them Steven wanted to ride on one they ran away pretty fast

Sunday 1 June

The sun came out this morning it's been really hot we went for a long walk and we found some interesting-looking mushrooms we decided NOT to cook them we don't want to risk being poisoned Zelda's parents are coming to collect us at five o'clock it's been a good weekend but I've had to do most of the work I seem to be the only sensible one here I suppose I'm a natural leader

COLiN'S CHALKBOARD CONCLUSIONS

SENTENCES

1. Every sentence needs a subject and a verb.

2. Every sentence needs an end stop.

3. Try combining short, jerky sentences in different ways.

4. Always take time drafting and redrafting important pieces of written work.

Remember, sentences can be short and pithy like, "He who hesitates is lost".

Or long: "He who forgets to write down the directions and loses the map is in a number of serious difficulties, too".

But the most important advice is — DON'T BE LIKE COLIN.

Oi!

SOME MISTAKES PEOPLE MAKE

accept / except

We **accept** your invitation with great pleasure. (verb)
Everyone was there **except** Ann. (preposition)

They all wanted to accept Colin.   **They all wanted to, except Colin.**

affect / effect

Winning the lottery will not **affect** my life. (verb)
The **effect** of the medicine was immediate. (noun)

allowed / aloud

Are we **allowed** to bring our pets? (verb)
Read your poem **aloud** to the class. (adverb)

Not allowed to speak aloud

are / our

Are you happy now? (verb)
They've been **our** friends for ages. (adjective)

as / has

Could you close the door **as** you leave? (conjunction)
Hugo **has** huge hands. (verb)

bought / brought

Have you **bought** all your Christmas presents yet? (verb – to buy)
We **brought** the plants to school in carrier bags. (verb – to bring)

**I bought you a present,
I haven't brought it.**

It brought me.

breath / breathe

I need a **breath** of fresh air. (noun)
Breathe deeply and fill those lungs. (verb)

buy / by

Where can I **buy** British bacon in Bradford? (verb)
This book is written **by** a friend of mine. (preposition)

did / done
i did my homework
i have done my homework

does / dose

Mrs. Green **does** annoy me. (rhymes with fuzz) (verb)
Here's your **dose** of vitamins. (rhymes with gross) (preposition)

draw / drawer

You can **draw** cars beautifully. (verb)
The bottom **drawer** of the chest is jammed. (noun)

Quick on the drawer

hear / here

Can you **hear** me at the back? (verb)
I'm over **here** by the window. (adverb)

> I can hear you, but I'll change places with someone in here who can't.

Very Old Jokes of the World, no. 53

lay / lie (verbs)

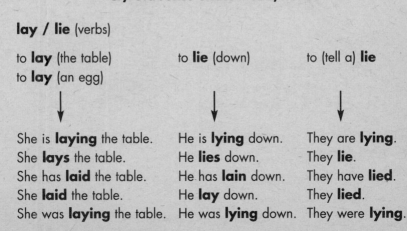

to **lay** (the table)	to **lie** (down)	to (tell a) **lie**
to **lay** (an egg)		
↓	↓	↓
She is **laying** the table.	He is **lying** down.	They are **lying**.
She **lays** the table.	He **lies** down.	They **lie**.
She has **laid** the table.	He has **lain** down.	They have **lied**.
She **laid** the table.	He **lay** down.	They **lied**.
She was **laying** the table.	He was **lying** down.	They were **lying**.

licence / license

You need a **licence**. (noun)
The village hall isn't **licensed** for a bar. (verb)

I'm waiter. A waiter.

Licensed to bill

lightening / lightning

They are **lightening** the load. (verb)
The **lightning** lit up the night sky. (noun)

like / as

You look **like** your father. (preposition)
As I told you, everything will be all right. (conjunction)
You look **as if** you've seen a ghost. (conjunction)

loose / lose

Shall I pull out that **loose** tooth? (adjective)
Don't **lose** your temper with me! (verb)

no / now / know

No, I won't come with you. (opposite of yes) (adverb)
Now I understand. (adverb)
Do you **know** when we break up? (verb)

of / off

She's the proud mother **of** ten children. (preposition)
Turn the light **off**. (adverb)

passed / past

Everyone has **passed** the exam. (verb)
She rushed **past** me. (preposition)

The ghost of Christmas Past   **The ghost of Christmas passed.**

practice / practise

An hour's **practice** every day is essential. (noun)
Practise the exercises every day. (verb)

SOME MISTAKES PEOPLE MAKE

principal / principle

My **principal** reason for taking the job is the money. (adjective)
Mrs Green is **Principal**. (= principal teacher)
I won't bet on **principle**. (noun)

I won't bet on Principal.

quiet / quite

You're so **quiet** that I thought you were asleep. (adjective)
I feel **quite** pleased at the result. (adverb)

stationary / stationery

Was the car **stationary** when you crashed into it? (adjective)
I usually give her **stationery** at Christmas. (noun)

seen / saw
I saw that
I have seen that

to / too / two

Would you like **to** go **to** the cinema? (prepositions)
You've given me far **too** much **too**. (adverb)
I've lost **two** pencils today. (adjective)

> One lost two games too.

> One would've liked to have won one.

weather / whether

It all depends on the **weather**. (noun)
I don't know **whether** you agree. (conjunction)

who / whom

He is the man **who** sold me the bicycle. (pronoun)
(= He is the man. <u>He</u> sold me the bicycle.)
He is the man **whom** you described. (pronoun)
or He is the man you described.
(= He is the man. You described <u>him</u>. It is acceptable to leave out
the word *whom* altogether in this sentence.)
Who sold you the bicycle? (Answer: <u>he</u> did) (pronoun)
Whom did you describe? (Answer: I described <u>him</u>) (pronoun)

Using *whom* may sound old-fashioned sometimes, but it does have
a different meaning to *who* and you should take care to use the
right word, especially when you are writing.

The Grammar Repair Kit M.O.T.
(Master/Mistress of Things) Certificate

This Certificate is awarded to

_____

in recognition of his/her fantastic achievement. Not
only can he/she now handle pronouns (like "he" and
"she") but also nouns (like "achievement"), adjectives
(like "fantastic", man) and verbs ("is", obviously) and
will never need to be tense about tenses, apologetic
about apostrophes or get conjunctivitis over
conjunctions – a singular achievement for someone
whose talents are now plural.

He/she need never again look stupid.
Well, grammatically speaking anyway. (Is there any
other way?)

Signed

Zelda

Colin

Steven

Why-Baby

Clevertrousers

Stanley Savenergy

ANSWERS

(page numbers are in brackets)

NOUNS
FIND THE WORDS – WIN A TROPHY (8)

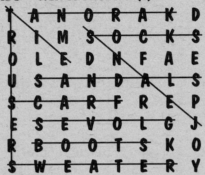

NAME THE BREED (9)
1. alsatian
2. poodle
3. sheepdog
4. bulldog
5. spaniel

HUNT THE PROPER NOUNS (13)
Manchester, Wales, Oliver, Norway, Everest

GENERAL KNOWLEDGE QUIZ (13)
1. Roald Dahl
2. William
3. Stockholm
4. Thor
5. January, February, March, April etc etc. All of them. This is a trick question, which is why the Proper Little Devil was there. All the months have 28 days – some have even more!

COLLECTIVE STRENGTH TEST (14)
1. flock
2. fleet / convoy
3. galaxy / constellation
4. shoal
5. gang

ANSWERS

VERY ADVANCED GRAMMATICAL POINT (17)
1. is
2. was
3. is
4. were
5. was

MEMO TO TROOPS (17)
is, is, realises

ENDINGS (18)
1. friendship
2. nervousness
3. boyhood
4. kingdom
5. loyalty
6. excitement
7. justice
8. failure
9. cruelty
10. gentleness

TESTING, TESTING (19)
1. loneliness
2. misery
3. confidence
4. generosity
5. cowardice
6. laziness
7. pride
8. width
9. bravery
10. nobility
11. beauty

GENDER-AL KNOWLEDGE (21)
MASCULINE: nephew, ram, bull, grandfather
FEMININE: nun, heiress, daughter, queen
COMMON: judge, doctor, pet, teacher
NEUTER: chair, book, telephone, desk

STAND-INS (21)

1. head / head teacher / principal
2. priest / vicar / cleric / member of the clergy
3. supervisor / work leader / team leader
4. police officer / police constable
5. spokesperson / representative / leader

PECULIAR PLURALS (26)

The two words in the singular are mouse and man. Their plurals are MICE and MEN.

EPONYMS (31)

1. nicotine
2. teddy bear
3. guillotine
4. biro
5. sandwich
6. JCB

PRONOUNS

CHOOSE THE RIGHT PRONOUN (34)

1. me
2. we
3. me
4. they
5. she

I OR ME (35)

1. I
2. me
3. me
4. I
5. me

CHECK THAT YOU UNDERSTAND (36)
1. his   yours
2. theirs   mine

WORDS AND DERIVATIONS (40)

bungalow	–	(Hindi) Bengal thatched house
dandelion	–	(French) lion's tooth
dinghy	–	(Hindi) a small boat
ketchup	–	(Malay) fish sauce
khaki	–	(Urdu & Persian) dusty
patio	–	(Spanish) a courtyard
pyjamas	–	(Hindustani) leg clothing
robot	–	(Czech) compulsory labour
spaghetti	–	(Italian) little strings
spider	–	(Old English) a spinner
terminus	–	(Latin) end, limit
thug	–	(Hindi) robber, murderer
vermicelli	–	(Italian) little worms

ADJECTIVES

STAMP OUT THE EVIL INTRUDER (42)
1. bed
2. apple
3. across
4. car
5. myself

SPELLING QUIZ (45)
15   fifteen
40   forty
90   ninety
5th   fifth
8th   eighth
12th   twelfth

SPOT TEST (47)
1. who's
2. whose
3. whose
4. who's
5. whose

SPOT CHECK (47)
1. its
2. its
3. it's
4. its
5. it's

AMERICANISMS (52)
1. biscuits   2. draughts   3. quilt
4. pedestrian crossing   5. pack   6. nappy   7. lift
8. autumn   9. tap   10. bumper
11. dustbin / rubbish bin   12. petrol   13. bonnet
14. flyover   15. baby's dummy   16. trousers
17. handbag   18. pavement   19. pushchair   20. boot

VERBS
ROADSIDE CHECK (55)
1. hate
2. punched
3. are
4. eats
5. bought
6. swallow

TEST YOUR UNDERSTANDING (55)
(possible answers)
1.   Give me a kiss. (noun)
     Kiss your mother. (verb)
2.   Do some work. (noun)
     Work harder. (verb)
3.   Your help has been valuable. (noun)
     Help! (verb)
4.   I had a dream last night. (noun)
     We dream every night. (verb)
5.   We went for a long walk. (noun)
     Walk faster. (verb)

DICTIONARY WORK (55)
widen
purify
specialise
beautify
fabricate

YOUR SHOUT (56)
1. was shouting
2. used to shout
3. shouted
4. have shouted

RIGHT OR WRONG (57)
1. X
2. X
3. X
4. X
5. X (Well, it was Steven)

DO IT YOURSELF (57)
1. woken
2. spoke
3. frozen
4. tried
5. thought

AUXILIARY VERBS (60)
1. do look
2. shall go
3. have forgotten
4. was snoring
5. is learning
6. have been / had been
7. has / had
8. was
9. shall / will
10. do / did

WIN A TROPHY NOW! (63)

1. . . . I'll feel
2. It's quite true . . .
3. can't . . . that's
4. we're . . .weren't
5. ✓
6. Didn't . . . they'd
7. ✓
8. you're
9. must've
10. ✓

SPANNERS AT THE READY (67)

1. When you walk round the corner, my cottage is on the left.
2. When she was skipping happily across the road, a bicycle nearly knocked her over.
3. Mary Poppins lived in the London of the 1890s which was famous for ill-health and muggings.

ADVERBS

ADD AN ADVERB (70-71)

(Other answers are possible for 1-5.)
1. softly   2. neatly   3. quickly   4. truly   5. firmly
6. safely   7. carefully   8. merrily   9. sincerely
10. really   11. often   12. least   13. slowly
14. never   15. tightly   16. enigmatically   17. stupidly
18. properly   19. strangely   20. beautifully   21. fiercely

PREPOSITIONS

SPOT THE DIFFERENCE (78)

1. drop in – visit unexpectedly, arrive casually
   drop out – give up, withdraw
2. laugh at – jeer, sneer, ridicule
   laugh off – treat something (like an injury) as if it doesn't matter
3. give away – give for no charge / betray
   give up – abandon, surrender, stop trying

CHOOSE THE RIGHT PREPOSITION (79)
1. about
2. for
3. to
4. with
5. up

CONJUNCTIONS AND INTERJECTIONS

AND, BUT, OR (81)
1. but
2. or
3. and

Zelda: I know the things I want to do to Colin and I have the right machinery, but all are either illegal or not painful enough.

PUT THAT SENTENCE RIGHT (82)
Steven is not only lazy but also greedy.

CHOOSE A CONJUNCTION (83)
6. as/while
7. as/before/after/when
8. when/if/whether
9. because/as/since/for
10. wherever

OI! YOU! NOW! (84)
1. (Express pain.)
2. (Express delight.)
3. (Express surprise.)
4. (Express disgust.)
5. (Express delight and surprise.)

SENTENCES

FIND THE SENTENCES (91)
2. He was very cross.
3. My mother gave me 50p.
8. You must be joking.

A QUESTIONABLE COMMAND PERFORMANCE (93)

1. My father ordered me to blow my nose.
2. My mother told my sister to get up.
3. My teacher asked me whether / if I was feeling better.
4. The old lady asked the shopkeeper how much the tomatoes were / the cost of the tomatoes / the price of the tomatoes.
5. My little brother asked me to tie his shoelaces / if I would tie his shoe laces / whether I would tie his shoelaces.

ROADSIDE CHECK (99)

As a half-term treat, Steven, Colin and Zelda are going camping in the New Forest ⊙ Fortunately they've been able to borrow a tent, a groundsheet and a campingstove ⊙ They already have warm sleeping bags ⊙ All week, it seems, they have been making lists, buying last-minute items, and packing rucksacks ⊙ The weather forecast is not very good but they'll enjoy themselves whatever the weather, if I know them.

COLIN'S DIARY (100)

(alternative punctuation in brackets)

Friday 30 May

We managed to get the tent up. (!) Steven wasn't much help. (!) It's lucky that I know something about camping. (!) Zelda forgot to pack the mallet. Fortunately I thought of using a tin of baked beans to bang the tent pegs in with. What would they do without me? They've got no ideas of their own. (!)

Saturday 31 May

It rained all night. (!) Luckily our sleeping bags are still dry. It was Steven's turn to cook today. We had a dreadful breakfast. (!) What will he be giving us tonight? The New Forest ponies are very timid. Can you blame them? Steven wanted to ride on one. (!) They ran away pretty fast!

Sunday 1 June

The sun came out this morning. It's been really hot. We went for a long walk and we found some interesting-looking mushrooms. We decided NOT to cook them. (!) We don't want to risk being poisoned. (!) Zelda's parents are coming to collect us at five o'clock. It's been a good weekend but I've had to do most of the work. I seem to be the only sensible one here. (!) I suppose I'm a natural leader. (!)

INDEX

BOOKS IN THE SERIES

0 340 89336 2	Grammar Repair Kit	£4.99
0 340 80499 8	Vocabulary Repair Kit	£4.99
0 340 89334 6	Punctuation Repair Kit	£4.99
0 340 77838 5	Science Repair Kit	£3.99
0 340 89335 4	Spelling Repair Kit	£4.99